TopReaders

Pompeii:
A Lost City

Sally Odgers

Contents

Mount Vesuvius is a volcano in Italy. In AD 79, it erupted, covering the cities of Pompeii and Herculaneum in ash. The world forgot about them. Centuries later, they were discovered again.

A Bustling City

In the first century, Pompeii was a rich and lively city in western Italy. Pompeiians loved to visit the forum and the public baths . There were many shops and fountains.

Everyday Life

Many of the people of Pompeii were wealthy. They lived in large villas and wore rich clothes. They could live like this partly because they had slaves to do the work.

peacock

Wealthy people ate fancy meals with many courses. One special meal was a roast peacock with live birds inside. When the peacock was carved at the table, the birds would fly out.

Warning Signs

Sometimes Pompeiians noticed small earth tremors . An earthquake in AD 62 did so much damage that repairs were still being made 17 years later.

fountain

A few days before Mount Vesuvius erupted, cracks appeared
in stone walls. Some of the water fountains stopped
flowing. The paving broke on the roads.
People were uneasy,
but not yet afraid.

cracked
wall

Eruption in Pompeii

On August 24, AD 79, Mount Vesuvius erupted in a huge, mushroom-shaped cloud of smoke and ash. Hot pumice and ash rained down over the city. Some Pompeiians fled, trying to save their belongings. Others stayed inside.

Fact File

Until the eruption of AD 79, the people of Pompeii did not know Mount Vesuvius was a volcano.

There was great destruction in Pompeii because it was right in the path of the eruption. People died when buildings collapsed, or from the hot ash and poisonous gas.

Eruption in Herculaneum

The coastal city of Herculaneum lay to the west of Mount Vesuvius. At first, only a little ash fell on Herculaneum. Many people escaped. Others took shelter in boathouses.

Later, gas and rock poured from the eruption in a pyroclastic flow . The intense heat of hot mud killed people instantly. Others died as they tried to escape in boats. Most of the buildings stayed intact, but they were buried in ash.

Under the Ash

The eruption of Mount Vesuvius covered Herculaneum in 66 feet (20 m) of volcanic deposits . Pompeii lay under more than 10 feet (3 m) of ash. Other cities and outlying villas were also destroyed.

Disaster Sites

This diagram shows the level of volcanic deposits in the two main cities.

level of volcanic deposits

Herculaneum   Pompeii

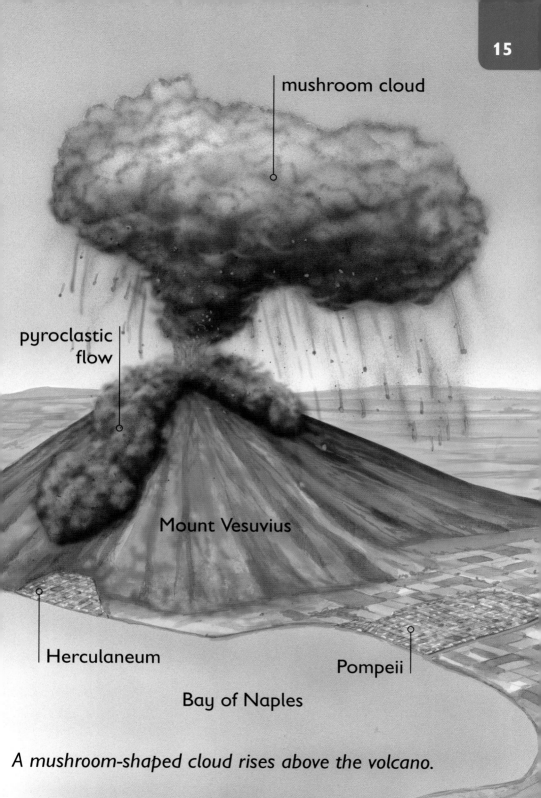

mushroom cloud

pyroclastic
flow

Mount Vesuvius

Herculaneum

Pompeii

Bay of Naples

A mushroom-shaped cloud rises above the volcano.

Witness of Disaster

Pliny the Younger saw the eruption from across the Bay of Naples and wrote an eyewitness account. His uncle, Pliny the Elder, died while trying to rescue friends.

Disaster Sites

Many people died in Herculaneum's boathouses as they waited for boats to save them. The people who escaped saw what happened to their cities.

The Bay of Naples was rough because of the eruption. Pliny wrote that the eruption had an umbrella-like shape.

☆**Fact File**
Like his uncle,
Pliny the Younger
was a famous
Roman writer.

Reactions in Rome

In Rome, about 150 miles (240 km) from the eruption, the new emperor , Titus, was in charge of the Roman Senate .

When Titus heard of the disasters,
he helped the people who had survived.

Emperor Titus

Survivors Return

The day after the eruption, survivors returned to find Pompeii buried. A hard crust like concrete had formed over the ash. Their city was gone forever, so the people went to live elsewhere.

Only the tops of
the tallest buildings
were visible.

Pompeii Today

Centuries passed. Pompeii was forgotten. Any artifacts found led to stories of a place called *la città* (the city). In the 18th century, someone discovered Herculaneum while digging a well. Pompeii was found soon after.

Fact File

Because of Pompeii and Herculaneum, scientists know a lot about everyday life in the first century.

Since 1748, *excavation* *of both sites has continued. Today, the excavations of Pompeii are important to scientists and to tourists.*

Plaster Models

The ash and hot mud preserved many of the bodies in Pompeii and Herculaneum. Scientists filled the cavities left by the bodies with plaster to make models of the people as they were when they died.

Making the Models

(1) After the eruption, a dead body is covered by ash.

(2) The ash is removed. The body is covered with plaster.

(3) The plaster sets and leaves a perfect cast of the body.

★ ★
☆ **Fact File**
Some of the plaster
casts are displayed
where the people
died. Others are
in museums.

House of the Vetti

The House of the Vetti belonged to two wealthy brothers in Pompeii. It is one of the best preserved buildings yet discovered. Tourists can visit the house and imagine what it was like to live there.

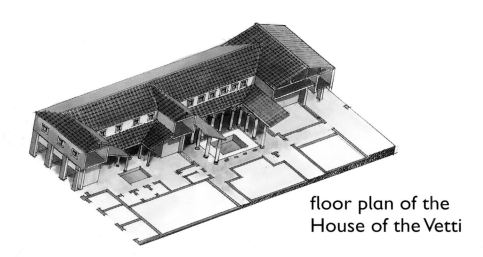

floor plan of the House of the Vetti

The two-story house has an atrium *, or inner courtyard, that is open to the sky. It is decorated with* frescoes *. These wall paintings show images of the sea, wine-making, and myths.*

Amazing Discoveries

Mosaics and jewelry are just two kinds of treasure that have been found in Pompeii. Because the end came suddenly, bread was left in ovens. Even dishes of olives were preserved under the ash.

dish of olives

These gold rings were found still on the finger of the owner's skeleton. The person died on one of Herculaneum's streets.

Quiz

Can you unscramble the words and match them with the right pictures?

HISD FO SILEVO   SUHEO FO ETH TIVET

LOCOVAN   RALSTEP LODEM

Glossary

artifacts: objects made by people

atrium: the central room in a Roman house

emperor: the ruler of an empire

erupted: forced out or released something

excavation: careful digging up of items or places

forum: a Roman meeting place

frescoes: paintings made on wet plaster

mosaics: pictures made by arranging tiles or pebbles in patterns

Pompeiians: people who lived in Pompeii

public baths: In Roman times, people met at the baths.

pumice: volcanic glass. Pumice is light, rough, and porous like a sponge.

pyroclastic flow: a stream of mud, rock, and gas that flows from a volcano

Senate: a group of important Roman citizens

survivors: people who live through a disaster

tremors: mild shakings or vibrations

villas: fine houses

volcanic deposits: lava, rock, pumice, and ash that come out of a volcano

volcano: a mountain over a weak spot in Earth's crust

Index